PREFACE

Bismillah,

In the gentle whispers of our hearts, whatever age we are, we often find emotions too profound for words. "A Pocketbook Full of Duas" is a small treasure crafted to resonate with the simplicity of your everyday moments. Duas can be the keys that unlock our hearts and connect us with the Almighty in times of joy, gratitude, sadness and even uncertainty.

This pocket-sized collection is here to be your companion, a guide to express your feelings in the language of prayer. Whether you're feeling grateful, anxious, or seeking strength, these Duas are like secret notes passed between you and Allah SWT, your confidant in every emotion.

As you turn the pages of this pocketbook, may you find comfort in knowing that your feelings are heard, understood, and cherished by the Most Merciful. May these Duas become a gentle reminder that, in the simplicity of prayer, we discover profound connections with the Divine.

May your journey with this pocketbook be one of closeness to Allah SWT, a whispered conversation in the language of the heart.

If there are any mistakes in this book, it is not intentional, Allah SWT please forgive me.

In the protection of Allah SWT,

Kayzy

I feel..

ANGRY

أَعُوْذُ بِاللهِ مِنَ الشَّيْطَانِ الرَّجِيْمِ

"I seek protection in Allah from the rejected Shayṭān"

Aʿūdhu bi-llāhi mina-sh-Shayṭāni-r-rajīm.

Allah says: "When you recite the Quran, seek refuge with Allah from rejected Shayṭān." (Quran 16:98)

I feel..

ANTICIPATION

اللهم إن كان هذا الأمر خيرا لي فَاقْدُرْهُ لِي وَيَسِّرْهُ لِي ثُمَّ بَارِكْ لِي فِيهِ

"Oh Allah, if my intended action is best for me, make it destined and easy for me, and grant me Your Blessings in it."

Allahumma in kaana haaza alAmr khayran lee fa iQdirhu lee wa yassirhu lee summa baarik lee feehi.

I feel..

ANXIOUS

حَسْبِيَ اللَّهُ لَا إِلَهَ إِلَّا هُوَ ، عَلَيْهِ تَوَكَّلْتُ ، وَهُوَ رَبُّ الْعَرْشِ الْعَظِيمِ

" Allah is sufficient for me. There is no god worthy of worship except Him. I have placed my trust in Him only and He is the Lord of the Magnificent Throne."

Ḥasbiya-Allāhu lā ilāha illā Huwa, ʿalayhi tawakkaltu, wa Huwa Rabbu-l-ʿArshi-l-ʿaẓīm.

Abū al-Dardāʾ (raḍiy Allāhu ʿanhu) narrates from the Messenger of Allah ﷺ at he said: "Whoever recites [the above] seven times in the morning and in the evening, Allah will suffice him in everything that concerns him in matters of this world and the next." (Ibn al-Sunnī 71)

I feel..

BORED

رَبِّ إِنِّي لِمَا أَنزَلْتَ إِلَيَّ مِنْ خَيْرٍ فَقِيرٌ

"My Lord, truly I am in dire need of any good which You may send me. (28:24)"

Rabbi innī limā anzalta illayya min khayrin faqīr.

I feel..

CONFIDENT

رَبِّ أَوْزِعْنِيٓ أَنْ أَشْكُرَ نِعْمَتَكَ الَّتِيٓ أَنْعَمْتَ عَلَيَّ وَعَلَىٰ وَالِدَيَّ وَأَنْ أَعْمَلَ صَالِحًا تَرْضَاهُ ، وَأَدْخِلْنِي بِرَحْمَتِكَ فِي عِبَادِكَ الصَّالِحِينَ

"My Lord, enable me to be grateful for Your favour which You have bestowed upon me and upon my parents, and to do good deeds that please You. And admit me by Your mercy amongst Your righteous servants. (27:19)"

Rabbi awziʿnī an ashkura niʿmataka-l-latī anʿamta ʿalayya wa ʿalā wālidayya wa an aʿmala ṣāliḥan tarḍāh, wa adkhilnī bi-raḥmatika fī ʿibādika-ṣ-ṣāliḥīn.

I feel..

CONFUSED

رَبِّ إِنِّي لِمَا أَنْزَلْتَ إِلَيَّ مِنْ خَيْرٍ فَقِيرٌ

"My Lord, truly I am in dire need of any good which You may send me. (28:24)"

Rabbi innī limā anzalta illayya min khayrin faqīr.

I feel..

CONTENT

اَللّٰهُمَّ مَا أَصْبَحَ بِيْ مِنْ نِّعْمَةٍ أَوْ بِأَحَدٍ مِّنْ خَلْقِكَ ، فَمِنْكَ وَحْدَكَ لَا شَرِيْكَ لَكَ ، فَلَكَ الْحَمْدُ وَلَكَ الشُّكْرُ

"O Allah, all the favours that I or anyone from Your creation has received in the morning, are from You Alone. You have no partner. To You Alone belong all praise and all thanks."

Allāhumma mā aṣbaḥa bī min niʿmatin aw bi-aḥadim-min khalqik, fa-minka waḥdaka lā sharīka lak, fa laka-l-ḥamdu wa laka-sh-shukr.

Abū al-Dardā' (raḍiy Allāhu 'anhu) narrates from the Messenger of All'Abdullāh b. Ghannām (raḍiy Allāhu 'anhu) narrates that the Messenger of Allah ﷺ said: "Whoever says [the above] in the morning has fulfilled his obligation to thank Allah for that day. And whoever says it in the evening has fulfilled his obligation for that night."
(Abū Dāwūd 5073)

I feel..

CURIOUS

اللهم إني أعوذ بك من شر سمعي، ومن شر بصري، ومن شر لساني، ومن شر قلبي، ومن شر منيي

"Oh Allah, I seek protection in you from the evil of my hearing, from the evil of my sight, from the evil of my tongue, from the evil of my heart, and from the evil of myself."

Allahumma inni a'uzubika min sharri sam'ee, wa min sharri basaree, wa min sharri lisaanee, wa min sharri qalbee, wa min sharri minnee.

I feel..

DEFEATED

اللهمّ إنّي ظلمت نفسي ظلماً كثيراً، ولا يغفر الذّنوب إلا أنت فاغفر لي مغفرة من عندك، وارحمني إنّك أنت الغفور الرّحيم

"O Allah, I have been very unjust to myself and no one grants pardon against sin but You, therefore forgive me with Your forgiveness and have mercy on me. Surely, You are the forgiver, the Merciful."

Allahumma Innee Dhalamtu nafsee Dhulman Kaseeran, Wa la yagfiru alZunuba illaa anta, fa igfirlee magfiratan min zndik, Wa Arhimnee, Innaka ant algafuur arraheem.

I feel..

DEPRESSED

حَسْبِيَ اللّٰهُ لَا إِلٰهَ إِلَّا هُوَ ، عَلَيْهِ تَوَكَّلْتُ ، وَهُوَ رَبُّ الْعَرْشِ الْعَظِيْمِ

"Allah is sufficient for me. There is no god worthy of worship except Him. I have placed my trust in Him only and He is the Lord of the Magnificent Throne."

Ḥasbiya-Allāhu lā ilāha illā Huwa, 'alayhi tawakkaltu, wa Huwa Rabbu-l-'Arshi-l-'aẓīm.

I feel..

DESPERATE

يا أرحم الراحمين أنتَ ربُّ المستضعفين وانت ربّي

"To You, my Lord, I complain of my weakness, lack of support and the humiliation I am made to receive. Most Compassionate and Merciful! You are the Lord of the weak, and you are my Lord."

Allahumma Innee Dhalamtu nafsee Dhulman Kaseeran, Wa la yagfiru alZunuba illaa anta, fa igfirlee magfiratan min i'ndika, Wa Arhimnee, Innaka ant algafuur arraheem.

I feel..

DETERMINED

اللهم امنحني القوة لأقاوم نفسي، والشجاعة لأواجه ضعفي، واليقين لأتقبل قدري، والرضا ليرتاح عقلي، والفهم ليطمئن قلبي

"Oh Allah! Grant me the strength to oppose myself, the courage to face my weakness, the conviction to accept my faith, the satisfaction of to relax my mind, and the understanding to reassure my heart."

Allahumma imnaHnee alQuwwah li aQwaami nafseee, wa ash-Shujaa'ah li uwaajih da3fee, wa alYaqeeni li ataQabbal qadree, wa ar-riDaa li yartaah 3aQalee, wa alfahm li yaTmainna Qalbee.

I feel...

DISBELIEF

اللهم املأ قلبي بحبك

"Oh Allah fill my heart with your love."

Allahumma imla' qalbee bihubbik.

I feel..

DOUBTFUL

اللهم إن كان هذا الأمر خيرا لي فَاقْدُرْهُ لِي وَيَسِّرْهُ لِي ثُمَّ بَارِكْ لِي فِيهِ

"Oh Allah, if my intended action is best for me, make it destined and easy for me, and grant me Your Blessings in it."

Allahumma in kaana haaza alAmr khayran lee fa iQdirhu lee wa yassirhu lee summa baarik lee feehi.

I feel..

ENVIOUS

اللهم طهر قلبي من كل سوء ، اللهم طهر قلبي من كل ما يبغضك، اللهم طهر قلبي من كل غلٍ وحقدٍ وحسد وكبر

"Oh Allah, clean away all forms of evil from my heart. Oh Allah, clean my heart and remove everything that displeases you. Oh Allah, clean my heart of all every form of bitterness, hard feelings, and jealousy."

Allahumma Tahhir Qalbee min kulli suu, Allahumma Tahhir Qalbee min kulli maa yubaGGiDuk. Allahumma Tahhir Qalbee min kulli Gillin wa HiQdin wa Hasadin wa kibr.

I feel..

GRATEFUL

اَللّٰهُمَّ مَا أَصْبَحَ بِيْ مِنْ نِّعْمَةٍ أَوْ بِأَحَدٍ مِّنْ خَلْقِكَ ، فَمِنْكَ وَحْدَكَ لَا شَرِيْكَ لَكَ ، فَلَكَ الْحَمْدُ وَلَكَ الشُّكْرُ

"O Allah, all the favours that I or anyone from Your creation has received in the morning, are from You Alone. You have no partner. To You Alone belong all praise and all thanks."

Allāhumma mā aṣbaḥa bī min niʿmatin aw bi-aḥadim-min khalqik, fa-minka waḥdaka lā sharīka lak, fa laka-l-ḥamdu wa laka-sh-shukr.

ʿAbdullāh b. Ghannām (raḍiy Allāhu ʿanhu) narrates that the Messenger of Allah said: "Whoever says [the above] in the morning has fulfilled his obligation to thank Allah for that day. And whoever says it in the evening has fulfilled his obligation for that night." (Abū Dāwūd 5073)

I feel..

GREEDY

اَللّٰهُمَّ قَنِّعْنِيْ بِمَا رَزَقْتَنِيْ ، وَبَارِكْ لِيْ فِيْهِ ، وَاخْلُفْ عَلَيَّ كُلَّ غَائِبَةٍ لِّيْ بِخَيْرٍ

"O Allah, make me content with what You have granted me, bless me in it and be a protector for me in that which is absent from me (i.e. family and wealth)."

Allāhumma qanninī bimā razaqtanī, wa bārik lī fīhī, wa-khluf ʿalā kulli ghā'ibati-l-lī bi-khayr.

I feel..

GUILTY

لَاۤ إِلٰهَ إِلَّاۤ أَنْتَ سُبْحَانَكَ إِنِّيْ كُنْتُ مِنَ الظَّالِمِيْنَ

"There is no god worthy of worship except You. You are free from imperfection. Indeed, I have been of the wrongdoers. (21:87)"

Lā ilāha illā Anta subḥānaka innī kuntu mina-ẓ-ẓālimīn.

I feel..

HAPPY

اَلْحَمْدُ لِلّٰهِ الَّذِيْ بِنِعْمَتِهِ تَتِمُّ الصَّالِحَاتُ

"All praise is for Allah through whose blessing righteous actions are accomplished."

Al-ḥamdu li-llāh-ladhī bi-niʿmatihī tattimmu-ṣ-ṣāliḥāt.

I feel..

HATRED

اللهم لا تجعل في قلبي كراهية لأحد

"Oh Allah, don't let the hate of anyone reside in my heart."

"Allahumma laa taj'al fee qalbee karaahiyyah li aHad."

I feel..

HUMILIATED

اللهم إليك أشكو ضعف قوتي وقلة حيلتي وهواني على الناس يا أرحم الراحمين أنت ربُّ المستضعفين وانت ربّي

"To You, my Lord, I complain of my weakness, lack of support and the humiliation I am made to receive. Most Compassionate and Merciful! You are the Lord of the weak, and you are my Lord."

"Allahuma ilayka ashku da'fa quwwati wa qillata heelatee wa hawanee 3ala an-naas ya arhamur rahimeen annta Rabbul mustad'afeen wa anta rabbi"

I feel..

HURT

اَللّٰهُمَّ رَحْمَتَكَ أَرْجُوْ فَلَا تَكِلْنِيْ إِلٰى نَفْسِيْ طَرْفَةَ عَيْنٍ، وَأَصْلِحْ لِي شَأْنِيْ كُلَّهُ لَا إِلٰهَ إِلَّا أَنْتَ

"O Allah! Your Mercy is what I hope for so do not entrust me to myself for the blink of an eye, rectify all of my affairs. There is no god worthy of worship but You."

Allāhumma raḥmataka ar jū fa-lā takilnī ilā nafsī ṭarfata ʿayn, wa aṣliḥ lī shaʾnī kullah lā ilāha illā Ant.

I feel..

HYPOCRITICAL

يَا مُقَلِّبَ الْقُلُوْبِ ثَبِّتْ قَلْبِيْ عَلَى دِيْنِكَ

"O Changer of the hearts, make my heart firm upon Your religion."

Yā Muqalliba-l-qulūbi thabbit qalbī ʿalā dīnik.

I feel..

IMPATIENT

يا صبور صبّرني على ما بلوتني وامتحنتني

"Oh The Most Patient, enable me to be patient upon whatever you afflict and test me with."

Ya Saboor Sabbirnee alaa maa balautanee wa imtaHantanee.

I feel..

INDECISIVE

اَللّٰهُمَّ أَلْهِمْنِيْ رُشْدِيْ ، وَأَعِذْنِيْ مِنْ شَرِّ نَفْسِيْ

"O Allah, inspire me with sound guidance and protect me from the evil of myself."

Allāhumma alhimnī rushdī, wa a'idhnī min sharri nafsī.

I feel..

INSECURE

اللهم اجعلني أرى المواهب و نقاط قوت الذين وضعته في نفسي

"Oh Allah, make me see the talents and strengths you have put inside of me."

Allahumma ijalnee araa almawaahib
wa nuqaat quwwat allazeena
wada'tahu fee nafsee.

I feel..

IRRITATED

اللهم طهر قلبي من كل سوء ، اللهم طهر قلبي من كل ما يبغضك، اللهم طهر قلبي من كل غلٍ وحقدٍ وحسد وكبر

"Oh Allah, clean away all forms of evil from my heart. Oh Allah, clean my heart and remove everything that displeases you. Oh Allah, clean my heart of all every form of bitterness, hard feelings, and jealousy."

Allahumma Tahhir Qalbee min kulli suu, Allahumma Tahhir Qalbee min kulli maa yubaghidhuk. Allahumma Tahhir Qalbee min kulli Gillin wa HiQdin wa Hasadin wa kibr.

I feel..

JEALOUS

رَبِّ أَعُوذُ بِكَ مِنْ هَمَزَاتِ الشَّيَاطِيْنِ ، وَأَعُوذُ بِكَ رَبِّ أَنْ يَّحْضُرُوْنِ

"My Lord, I seek protection with You from the promptings of the devils; and I seek protection in You, my Lord, from their coming near me. (23:97-98)"

Rabbi aūdhu bika min hamazāti-sh-shayāṭīn. Wa aūdhu bika Rabbi ay-yaḥḍurūn.

I feel..

LAZY

اَللّٰهُمَّ إِنِّي أَعُوذُ بِكَ مِنَ الْهَمِّ وَالْحَزَنِ ، وَأَعُوذُ بِكَ مِنَ الْعَجْزِ وَالْكَسَلِ، وَأَعُوذُ بِكَ مِنَ الْجُبْنِ وَالْبُخْلِ ، وَأَعُوذُ بِكَ مِنْ غَلَبَةِ الدَّيْنِ وَقَهْرِ الرِّجَالِ

"O Allah, I seek Your protection from anxiety and grief. I seek Your protection from inability and laziness. I seek Your protection from cowardice and miserliness, and I seek Your protection from being overcome by debt and being overpowered by men."

Allāhumma innī aūdhu bika min-l-hammi wa-l-ḥazan, wa aūdhu bika min-l-'ajzi wa-l-kasal, wa aūdhu bika min-l-jubni wa-l-bukhl, wa aūdhu bika min ghalabati-d-dayni wa qahri-r-rijāl.

I feel..

LONELY

حَسْبِيَ اللهُ لَا إِلٰهَ إِلَّا هُوَ ، عَلَيْهِ تَوَكَّلْتُ ، وَهُوَ رَبُّ الْعَرْشِ الْعَظِيْمِ

"Allah is sufficient for me. There is no god worthy of worship except Him. I have placed my trust in Him only and He is the Lord of the Magnificent Throne."

Ḥasbiya-Allāhu lā ilāha illā Huwa, ʿalayhi tawakkaltu, wa Huwa Rabbu-l-ʿArshi-l-ʿaẓīm.

I feel..

LOST

رَبِّ إِنِّي لِمَآ أَنزَلْتَ إِلَيَّ مِنْ خَيْرٍ فَقِيرٌ

"My Lord, truly I am in dire need of any good which You may send me. (28:24)"

Rabbi innī limā anzalta illayya min khayrin faqīr.

I feel..

NERVOUS

حَسْبِيَ اللّٰهُ لَا إِلٰهَ إِلَّا هُوَ ، عَلَيْهِ تَوَكَّلْتُ ، وَهُوَ رَبُّ الْعَرْشِ الْعَظِيْمِ

"Allah is sufficient for me. There is no god worthy of worship except Him. I have placed my trust in Him only and He is the Lord of the Magnificent Throne."

Ḥasbiya-Allāhu lā ilāha illā Huwa, 'alayhi tawakkaltu, wa Huwa Rabbu-l-'Arshi-l-'aẓīm.

I feel..

OFFENDED

اللهم إنِّي أَعُوذُ بِكَ مِنْ هَمٍّ يَحْزُنُنِي وَمِنْ فِكْرٍ يُقْلِقُنِي وَعِلْمَا يُتْعِبُنِي وَشَخْصًا يَحْمِلُ خُبْثًا لِي

"Oh Allah! I seek your shelter from worries that sadden me, thoughts that make me restless, information that bothers me, and people that intend bad for me."

Allahumma innee a'uzubika min ham ayhzununee, wa min fikr yuqliquneae, wa 3ilm yut3ibunee, wa shakhS yahmilu khubsan-lee

I feel..

OVERWHELMED

حَسْبِيَ اللّٰهُ لَا إِلٰهَ إِلَّا هُوَ ، عَلَيْهِ تَوَكَّلْتُ ، وَهُوَ رَبُّ الْعَرْشِ الْعَظِيْمِ

"Allah is sufficient for me. There is no god worthy of worship except Him. I have placed my trust in Him only and He is the Lord of the Magnificent Throne."

Ḥasbiya-Allāhu lā ilāha illā Huwa, 'alayhi tawakkaltu, wa Huwa Rabbu-l-'Arshi-l-'aẓīm.

I feel..

PEACEFUL

اللَّهُمَّ إِنِّي أَعُوذُ بِكَ مِنْ زَوَالِ نِعْمَتِكَ، وَتَحَوُّلِ عَافِيَتِكَ، وَفُجَاءَةِ نِقْمَتِكَ، وَجَمِيعِ سَخَطِكَ

"O Allah! I seek refuge in You from the decline of Your blessings, the passing of safety, the sudden onset of Your punishment and from all that displeases you."

Allahumma inni a'udhu bika min zawali ni'matika, wa tahawwuli 'afiyatika, wa fuja'ati niqmatika, wa jami'i sakhatika.

I feel..

RAGE

اللَّهُمَّ أَذْهِبْ غَيْظَ قَلْبِي

"Oh Allah, remove anger from my heart."

Allahumma azhib Gaydha Qalbee.

I feel..

REGRET

أَنْتَ وَلِيُّنَا فَاغْفِرْ لَنَا وَارْحَمْنَا ۖ وَأَنْتَ خَيْرُ الْغَافِرِينَ

"You are our Protector, so forgive us and have mercy upon us. You are the best of those who forgive. (7:155)"

Anta Walliyyunā fa-ghfir lanā war-ḥamnā wa Anta khayrul-ghāfirīn..

I feel..

SAD

رَبِّ إِنِّي لِمَا أَنزَلْتَ إِلَيَّ مِنْ خَيْرٍ فَقِيرٌ

"My Lord, truly I am in dire need of any good which You may send me. (28:24)"

Rabbi innī limā anzalta illayya min khayrin faqīr.

I feel..

SATISFIED

اللَّهُمَّ إِنِّي أَعُوذُ بِكَ مِنْ زَوَالِ نِعْمَتِكَ، وَتَحَوُّلِ عَافِيَتِكَ، وَفُجَاءَةِ نِقْمَتِكَ، وَجَمِيعِ سَخَطِكَ

"O Allah! I seek refuge in You from the decline of Your blessings, the passing of safety, the sudden onset of Your punishment and from all that displeases you."

Allahumma inni a'udhu bika min zawali ni'matika, wa tahawwuli 'afiyatika, wa fuja'ati niqmatika, wa jami'i sakhatika.

I feel..

SCARED

اَللّٰهُمَّ إِنَّا نَجْعَلُكَ فِيْ نُحُوْرِهِمْ ، وَنَعُوْذُ بِكَ مِنْ شُرُوْرِهِمْ

"O Allah, we make You our shield against them and we seek refuge in You from their evil."

Allāhumma innā najʿaluka fī nuḥūrihim, wa naʿūdhu bika min shurūrihim.

I feel..

TIRED

اَللّٰهُمَّ إِنِّي أَعُوْذُ بِكَ مِنَ الْهَمِّ وَالْحَزَنِ ، وَأَعُوْذُ بِكَ مِنَ الْعَجْزِ وَالْكَسَلِ، وَأَعُوْذُ بِكَ مِنَ الْجُبْنِ وَالْبُخْلِ ، وَأَعُوْذُ بِكَ مِنْ غَلَبَةِ الدَّيْنِ وَقَهْرِ الرِّجَالِ

"O Allah, I seek Your protection from anxiety and grief. I seek Your protection from inability and laziness. I seek Your protection from cowardice and miserliness, and I seek Your protection from being overcome by debt and being overpowered by men."

Allāhumma innī aʿūdhu bika min-l-hammi wa-l-ḥazan, wa aʿūdhu bika min-l-ʿajzi wa-l-kasal, wa aʿūdhu bika min-l-jubni wa-l-bukhl, wa aʿūdhu bika min ghalabati-d-dayni wa qahri-r-rijāl.

I feel..

UNCERTAIN

اللهم اغسلني من السلبية

"Oh Allah wash away my negativity."

"Allahumma Ghsilnee min assalbiyah"

I feel..

UNEASY

اللهم أنزِل عليّ سكينة من عندك تشرح بها صدري و تحفظُ بها قلبي

'Oh Allah, descend upon me satisfaction that comes from you and open my chest and protect my heart with it."

Allahumma Anzil alay sakeenah min andik tashrah bihaa Sadree wa tahfadh bihaa qalbee

I feel..

UNLOVED

$$\text{حَسْبُنَا اللّٰهُ وَنِعْمَ الْوَكِيْلُ}$$

"Allah is enough for us and He is the Best Protector."

Ḥasbunallāhu wa niʿmal Wakīl.

Ibn ʿAbbās (radiy Allāhū ʿanhumā) narrated: "[the above] was said by Ibrāhīm (ʿalayhis-salām) when he was thrown into the fire; and it when they (i.e. the hypocrites) said, "A was said by Muhammad great army is gathering against you, therefore, fear them," but it only increased their faith and they said: "Allah is Sufficient for us, and He is the Best Disposer (of affairs, for us)." (3.173)
(Bukhārī 4563)

I feel..

WEAK

اَللّٰهُمَّ لَا سَهْلَ إِلَّا مَا جَعَلْتَهُ سَهْلًا ، وَأَنْتَ تَجْعَلُ الْحَزْنَ إِذَا شِئْتَ سَهْلًا

"O Allah, there is no ease except in that which You have made easy, and You make the difficulty easy when You wish."

Allāhumma lā sahla illā mā ja'altahū sahlā, wa anta taj'alu-l-ḥazna idhā shi'ta sahlā.

Make me feel

BETTER

(اللهم شفني)

"O Allah, cure/heal me."

Allahumma shfi ni

I can't

CONCENTRATE

اللهم أعني على ذكرك وشكرك وحسن عبادتك

"O Allah, help me in remembering You, expressing gratitude to You, and in worshiping You excellently."

Allahumma a'inni 'ala dhikrika wa shukrika wa husni 'ibadatika.

help with

EXAMS

اللهم لا سهل إلا ما جعلته سهلاً، وأنت تجعل الحزن إذا شئت سهلاً

"O Allah, there is no ease except in what You have made easy. If You wish, You can make the difficult easy."

Allahumma la sahla illa ma ja'altahu sahlan, wa anta taj'alul huzna idha shi'ta sahlan.

make me feel

SAFE

اللهم إني أعوذ بك من كل شر، وأسألك الأمان يوم الأزلة.

"O Allah, I seek refuge in You from all evil, and I ask You for safety on the day of insecurity."

Allahumma inni a'udhu bika min kulli sharri, wa as'aluka al-amana yawma al-azillah.

I can't

SLEEP

اللَّهُمَّ غَارَتِ النُّجُومُ وَهَدَأَتِ الْعُيُونُ وَأَنْتَ حَيٌّ قَيُّومٌ * لَا تَأْخُذُكَ سِنَةٌ وَلَا نَوْمٌ يَا حَيُّ يَا قَيُّومُ أَهْدِئْ لَيْلِي وَأَنِمْ عَيْنِي

"O Allah the stars have gone far away and the eyes are rested. You are Alive and Infinite, You do not slumber nor does sleep overtake You. Oh Alive and the Everlasting One, grant me rest tonight and let my eyes sleep (close)."

Allahumma inna nujuma baghatin wa habsa al-aynu, anta al-Hayy al-Qayyum, la ta'khudhuka sinatun wa la nawm, ya Hayy ya Qayyum, ansurni ala man khalafa.

dua for

SOMEONE'S RECOVERY

اللهم رب الناس، أذهِب البأس، اشفِ أنت الشافي، لا شفاء إلا شفاؤك، شفاءً لا يغادر سقماً.

"O Allah, Lord of mankind, remove the affliction and cure, as You are the only One who cures. There is no cure but Your cure; a cure that leaves no illness."

Allahumma Rabb an-nas, adhhib al-ba's, ishf Anta ash-Shafi, la shifa'a illa shifa'uka, shifa'an la yughadiru saqaman.

AYATUL KURSI

اللَّهُ لَا إِلَٰهَ إِلَّا هُوَ الْحَيُّ الْقَيُّومُ ۚ لَا تَأْخُذُهُ سِنَةٌ وَلَا نَوْمٌ ۚ لَّهُ مَا فِي السَّمَاوَاتِ وَمَا فِي الْأَرْضِ ۗ مَن ذَا الَّذِي يَشْفَعُ عِندَهُ إِلَّا بِإِذْنِهِ ۚ يَعْلَمُ مَا بَيْنَ أَيْدِيهِمْ وَمَا خَلْفَهُمْ ۖ وَلَا يُحِيطُونَ بِشَيْءٍ مِّنْ عِلْمِهِ إِلَّا بِمَا شَاءَ ۚ وَسِعَ كُرْسِيُّهُ السَّمَاوَاتِ وَالْأَرْضَ ۖ وَلَا يَئُودُهُ حِفْظُهُمَا ۚ وَهُوَ الْعَلِيُّ الْعَظِيمُ

"Allah! There is no god ˹worthy of worship˺ except Him, the Ever-Living, All-Sustaining. Neither drowsiness nor sleep overtakes Him. To Him belongs whatever is in the heavens and whatever is on the earth. Who could possibly intercede with Him without His permission? He ˹fully˺ knows what is ahead of them and what is behind them, but no one can grasp any of His knowledge—except what He wills ˹to reveal˺. His Seat1 encompasses the heavens and the earth, and the preservation of both does not tire Him. For He is the Most High, the Greatest."

Allahu laaa ilaaha illaa huwal haiyul qai-yoom; laa taakhuzuhoo sinatunw wa laa nawm; lahoo maa fissamaawaati wa maa fil ard; man zallazee yashfa'u indahooo illaa be iznih; ya'lamu maa baina aideehim wa maa khalfahum; wa laa yuheetoona beshai 'immin 'ilmihee illa be maa shaaaa; wasi'a kursiyyuhus samaa waati wal arda wa la ya'ooduho hifzuhumaa; wa huwal aliyyul 'azeem.

AUTHOR'S NOTE

In creating "A Pocketful of Duas," I sought solace in the transformative power of supplication during a challenging time. I chose to conclude this book with the powerful Ayat al-Kursi, (Verse 255 of Surah-e-Baqarah (chapter: The cow)), a Dua that proved immensely helpful for my children and me during three difficult months. In a situation away from our home and the life we had taken for granted, faced with unforeseen difficulties, we turned to the profound words of Ayat al-Kursi each day. Without it, the children struggled to sleep, and it guided us through the toughest of times. It solidified my faith in Allah, and we felt protected by His presence.

This pocket-sized collection encapsulates not only the resilience we discovered within ourselves but also the universal comfort found in seeking refuge through prayer. As you embark on this journey of supplication, may these Duas become a source of peace and strength, just as they were for us.

May the whisper of these sacred words resonate within your heart, bringing serenity to your soul.

Warm regards,

Kayzy

Printed in Great Britain
by Amazon